Moloka'i

Maui

Iawai'i
e Big Island

To Vince and Lauren, my inspirations for this story.

— Sharon Lee Asta

To my Dad. Thanks for everything.

— Jeanne Uyehara Donovan

ABC's of Hawai'i
Written by Sharon Lee Asta & Jeanne Uyehara Donovan ©text
Illustrated by Alexis America

Produced and published by

ISLAND HERITAGE
P U B L I S H I N G

94-411 Kō'aki Street, Waipahu, Hawai'i 96797
Orders: (800) 468-2800 • Information: (808) 564-8800
Fax: (808) 564-8877 • www.islandheritage.com

ISBN 0-89610-346-3

First Edition, Eleventh Printing—2003

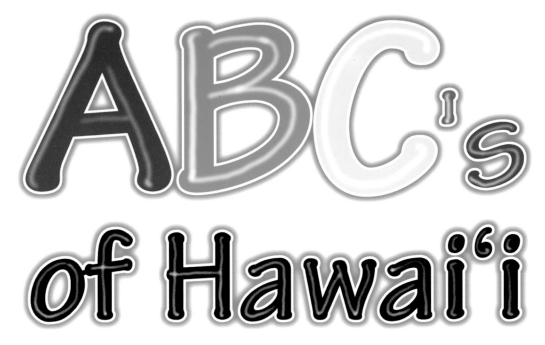

ABC's of Hawai'i

WRITTEN BY SHARON LEE ASTA & JEANNE UYEHARA DONOVAN
ILLUSTRATED BY ALEXIS AMERICA

ISLAND HERITAGE

Mariko is visiting Grandma in Hawai'i for the first time.
Her secret wish is to wear a flower necklace called a lei.
Maybe Grandma will buy her one.
Do you see a lei in the picture?

Aa is for Aloha

"Aloha — hello," says Grandma.
After she hugs Mariko, she gives her a candy lei.
"Welcome to Hawai'i, my Mariko."
Is this the lei in Mariko's secret wish?
Come search with her through the alphabet for the lei.

3

Bb

is for Beach

Shovel the sand.
Pat the sand.
Dig deeper and deeper.
Now, Mariko and Grandma can sit in the hole.
Why won't flowers grow on the beach?

Cc is for Coral

Mariko sees pretty colors underwater.
The colors are coral.
Coral lives and grows underwater.
Would Mariko find her lei down here?

Dd is for Diamond Head

Mariko is afraid to climb that famous mountain.
She squeezes Grandma's hand.
"Trust me," Grandma says. "Diamond Head is a dead volcano."
Will Mariko see any flowers growing high on the slope?

Ee

is for Eel

An eel hides between the rocks.
Mariko stares back at the eel in the tank.
No flowers here.
Where else should Mariko search for flowers?

is for Flowers

Mariko wants all these flowers in her lei.
"The flowers are not for picking,"
whispers Grandma. "They are for looking."
How do you think the Bird of Paradise
got its name?

G g

is for Guava

Grandma picks the guava
for Mariko.
Mariko feels sad.
She loves guava,
but the fruit is not a flower.
No lei here.
What will Mariko do now?

Hh is for Hula

Grandma and the dancers tell a story with their hands.
The hula skirt and lei are part of their costumes.
Mariko wonders if she must take hula lessons to get her lei.
Can you tell a story with your hands? Try it.

Ii is for Islands

Flowers grow everywhere on the
Hawaiian Islands.
Mariko's lei must be
here somewhere.
She will find it.
Keep searching, Mariko!
Look at a map.
Can you name
the biggest island?

Jj
is for Jellyfish

Grandma shows Mariko
how to fish from the rocky shore.
Mariko wants to hook the bubbles instead.
The bubbles look like flowers.
"Do not touch them," Grandma says.
"Those are jellyfish and they can sting you."
Why do you think they are called jellyfish?

Kk

is for Koi

Koi look like big goldfish.
Mariko thinks they float like flowers.
Flowers don't really swim.
How many colors can you see in the koi?
Draw and color a koi.

Ll

is for Lū'au

The drums are calling Mariko to this Hawaiian feast.
She and Grandma taste all the foods.
They eat with their fingers.
They even get to lick them!
Mariko wears a seashell lei tonight.
What do you eat with your fingers?

Mm

is for Muʻumuʻu

"Now, where is my Mariko?" teases Grandma.
Mariko sees flower patterns on
Grandma's muʻumuʻu.
She tries to pick them off the dress.
Grandma giggles.
How many flowers
can you count on
Mariko's muʻumuʻu?

Nn

is for Nut

A native girl, called a wāhine,
strings kukui nuts together
into a lei.
Mariko wonders if this is how
flower leis are made.
What part of the plant is the nut?

Oo

is for 'Ono

Mariko eats the shave ice.
"'Ono!" Grandma sings, happily.
"What does 'ono mean?" asks Mariko.
"Delicious!" answers Grandma.
The different colors of shave ice remind
Mariko of flowers.
Can you guess the flavors in
Mariko's cone?

P p is for Pineapple

Mariko cannot see the end of the pineapple field.
She imagines flowers growing
in rows like pineapples.
Can you draw a funny pineapple flower?

Qq

is for Queen

"Queen Lili'uokalani lived many years ago,"
says Grandma.
What pretty leis she has, Mariko thinks.
Mariko wants her lei to look just like the Queen's.
Do you think the lei was part of
the royal costume?

Rr

is for Rainbow

Mariko and Grandma dance under the rainbow.
Hawaiian showers smell of the rain forest.
Hawaiian showers help flowers grow, too.
Do you know the colors of the rainbow?
Name them.

Ss

is for Surfer

"Catch the wave!" Grandma shouts.
Mariko paddles her surfboard.
Where do you think the wave will take her?

Tt is for Tūtū

"Tūtū" is the Hawaiian word for "Grandma."
Tūtū helps Mariko string beads for a necklace.
Mariko pretends the beads are flowers.
What patterns do you see in Mariko's necklace?

27

Uu is for 'Ukulele

Mariko strums her 'ukulele in Grandma's garden.
A breeze dances through the flowers.
Mariko giggles when the leaves tickle
her shoulder.
Flowers smell like perfume.
Can you sing and smell
at the same time?
Try it.

Vv

is for Volcano

Kīlauea Volcano is quiet today.
Mariko stands by a warm lava flow.
The shiny crust smells like rotten eggs.
Mariko pinches her nose.
Her lei would not smell stinky.
What do you think smells bad?

29

Ww

is for Waikīkī

Waikīkī is a favorite beach in Honolulu. People come from far away to swim at Waikīkī.

But Mariko only sees people, not flowers. Where will she go now?

Xx

is for Mariko's footprints on the beach.
She jumps.
She hops.
She crawls.
Say the letter Mariko made.
Can you draw a flower out of this letter?

Yy

is for Yawn

Mariko has tasted, smelled, touched, seen and listened to Hawai'i.
She is too tired to remember all the places she visited.
Can you help her?

Zz

is for Zzzzz - snoring

Mariko returns home tomorrow.
Did she find her lei?
You will see when she wakes up.
Wake up, Mariko!

She heard you.
Snip, snip, snip.
Grandma fills a basket in the garden.
What does Mariko see?

"Tūtū!" Mariko cries. "I found my flowers!
They were here all the time.
Can you help me string my lei?"

35

Mahalo - Come back soon!

Kaua‘i

Ni‘ihau

O‘ahu

Lāna‘i

I
TH